# SPECTACULAR YOSEMITE

# SPECTACULAR YOSEMITE

Quang–Tuan Luong

*and*

Stuart Booth

UNIVERSE

This edition published in 2011 by
Published by Universe Publishing
A Division of Rizzoli Publishing
A Division of Rizzoli International Publications, Inc.
300 Park Avenue South
New York, NY 10010
*www.rizzoliusa.com*

ISBN-13: 978-0-7893-2224-1

Copyright © 2011 Compendium Publishing Ltd
43 Frith Street
London WC1V 4SA
United Kingdom

Library of Congress Control Number: 2010935637

Printed and bound in China

Project manager: Stuart Booth
Editor: Josh Rosenberg
Maps by Mark Franklin
Thanks to Patrick Nugent for significant design input

**PAGE 1** Yosemite Falls reflected in a run-off pond.

**TITLE PAGE** The Yosemite Valley towers above the Merced River in the fall.

**LEFT** In late afternoon light, remnants of ancient glaciers—called erratics—still stand undisturbed on Olmsted Point.

**OPPOSITE** Cathedral rocks and the Merced River with fresh snow.

**FOLLOWING PAGES** A classic view of Yosemite Valley in the early fall.

# CONTENTS

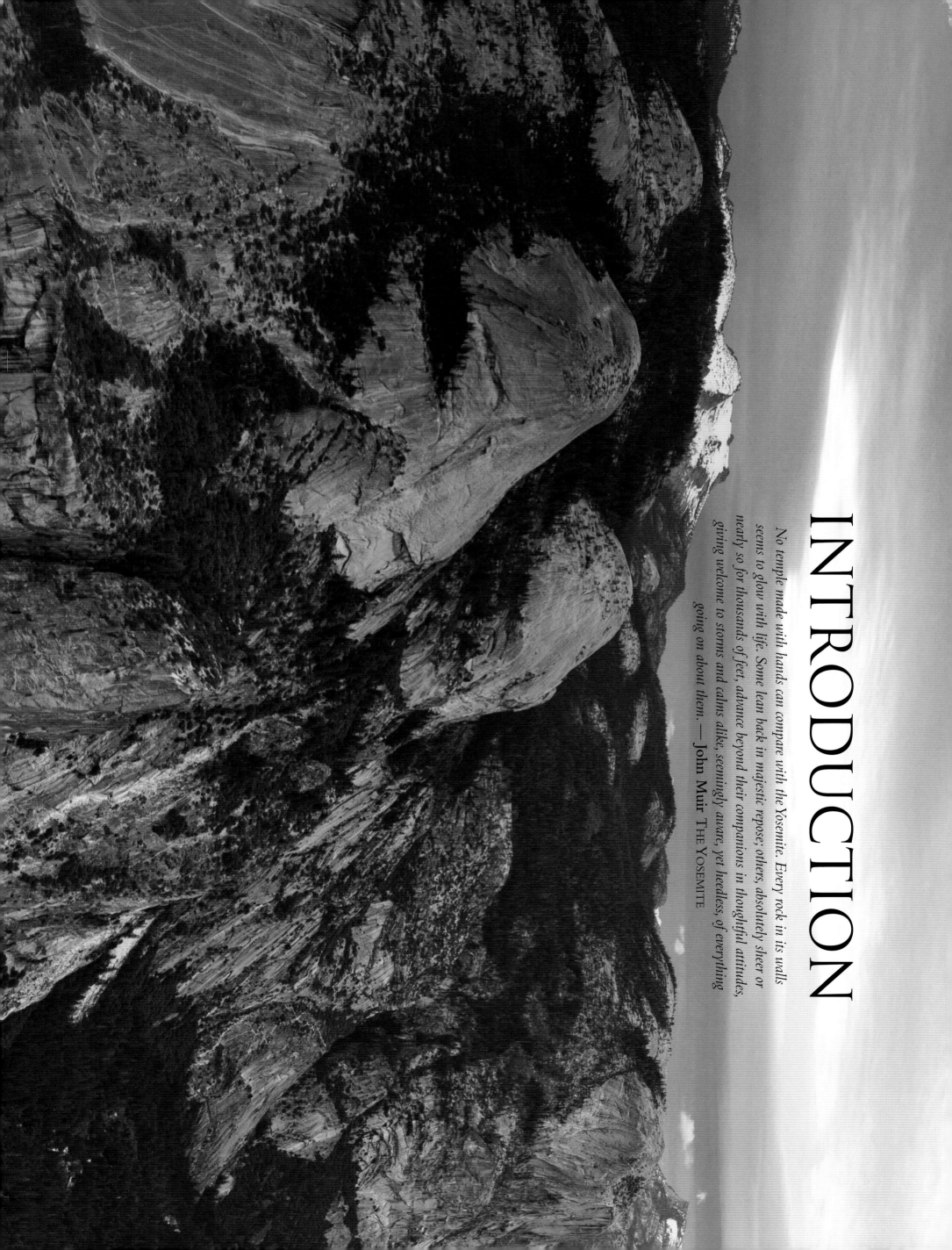

# INTRODUCTION

*No temple made with hands can compare with the Yosemite. Every rock in its walls
seems to glow with life. Some lean back in majestic repose; others, absolutely sheer or
nearly so for thousands of feet, advance beyond their companions in thoughtful attitudes,
giving welcome to storms and calms alike, seemingly aware, yet heedless, of everything
going on about them.* — **John Muir** The Yosemite

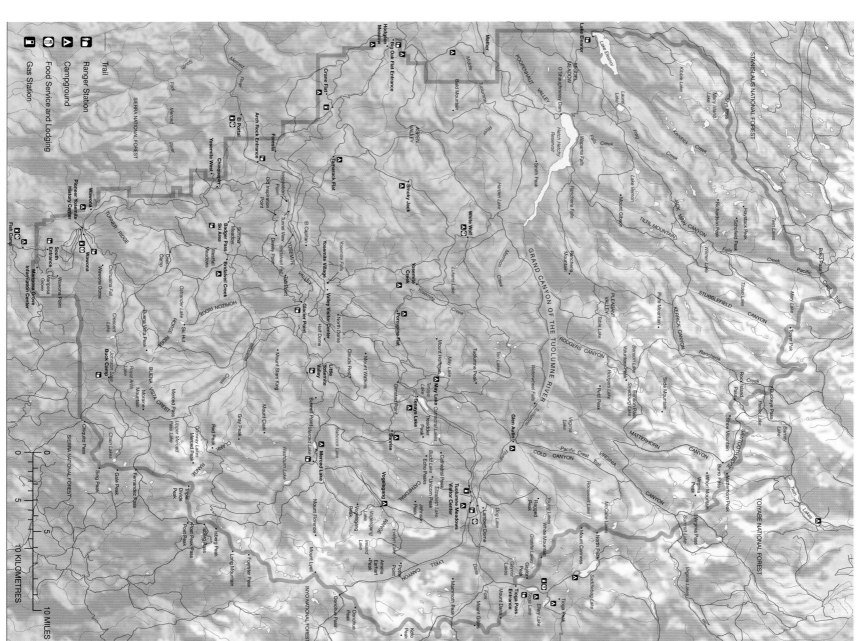

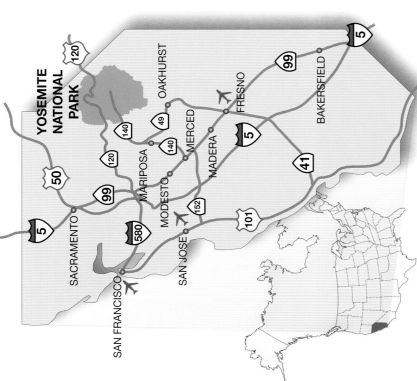

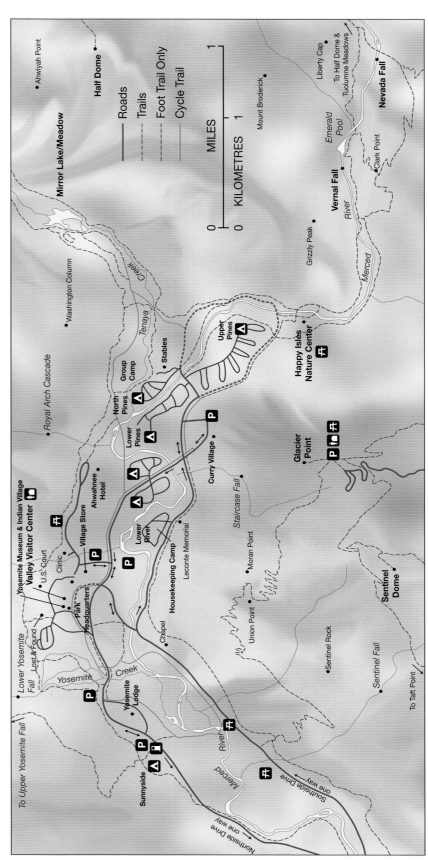

More glowing adjectives have been associated with Yosemite National Park than with any other scenic locale in the United States. Yet, however excessive the hyperbole can sometimes seem to be, once any visitor enters the Park via the Portal Route and turns the corner coming out of the rocky archway to see Yosemite Valley—only a small part of the Park, but one that attracts most of the gushing words—there is the immediate realization that all of the seeming exaggeration is actually understated. For many, Yosemite Valley is quite simply the single most dramatic natural location in the world.

Although a mere seven miles long and a mile across at its widest point, the Valley's walls are near-vertical cliffs—down the sides of which cascade spectacular waterfalls—and are surmounted by a variety of rocky domes and pinnacles, creating a jagged silhouette against the Sierra Nevada sky. At ground level, the sights can be just as impressive, with grassy meadows framed by oak, cedar, and fir trees. In addition, visitors may discover a variety of wildflowers and wildlife, such as coyotes and black bears. Quite understandably, tourist numbers have increased considerably over the years. But the Park as a whole is a diverse and massive enough area to accommodate the crowds. It is accessible any time of year—though less so in winter, when waterfalls turn to ice and snow-blocked trails force the closure of a large portion of the Park until the spring thaw. Even the Valley itself, other than in high summer, can be reasonably uncluttered. More remote parts of the Park, especially around the alpine habitat of the Tuolumne Meadows, are much less busy year-round—especially the almost virginally wild backcountry that is accessible beyond the meadows. Yosemite provides just about the most peaceful and elemental surroundings that any urban dweller might ever imagine.

## DISCOVERY AND NAMING

For many centuries the Paiute and Miwok Native American peoples lived in the eastern part of California's Central Valley and the western area of the Sierra Nevada, with a band of them called the Awani—or Ahwaneechee—occupying a secluded home that they called *ahwahnee*, or "deep grassy valley." There they enjoyed the security and natural abundance of the seven-mile valley defined by the immensely high granite sides, formed over the aeons by the action of water and glaciers.

It is possible that some members of Joseph Walker's forty-strong explorer team of 1833 entered the Valley as part of their Sierra expedition. Nevertheless, the "official" historical credit for discovery of this paradise is given to Major James D. Savage and Dr. Lafayette H. Bunnell. However, modern enlightened attitudes afford them no great purpose in this, as they were heading up U.S. troops of the Mariposa Battalion in pursuit of what they perceived as being hostile Miwok. As the troop emerged from a forest trail, it found itself at the head of a rocky promontory—known today as Inspiration Point—that overlooked the entire valley floor. A few years later, Bunnell

wrote: "As I looked at the grandeur of the scene, a peculiar exalted sensation seemed to fill my whole being and I found my eyes in tears of emotion." He went on to remember the grizzly bear, the valley totem of the Miwok and which they called *uzumati*; and so he named the valley Yosemite (pronounced "yo-SEM-it-ee"). Another explanation has Bunnell naming the valley from his interviews with Chief Tenaya, the founder of the Paiute Colony of Ah-wah-nee. The Miwok (and most settlers) considered the Ahwahneechee to be especially violent due to their frequent territorial disputes, and the Miwok word *yohhe'meti* means, literally, "they are killers." Whatever the origins of its name, correspondence and articles written by members of the battalion helped to popularize the valley and surrounding area. It eventually became Yosemite National Park, located in California's Mariposa, Tuolumne, and Madera Counties in the central Sierra Nevada. It is some three and a half hours from San Francisco and about six hours from Los Angeles, surrounded

**RIGHT AND OPPOSITE, RIGHT** The Yosemite National Park, its location (right), and the Yosemite Valley in detail (below).

**OPPOSITE, LEFT** Climbers flock to the spectacular faces of the Valley. This is El Capitan.

by the Ansel Adams Wilderness to the southeast, the Hoover Wilderness to the northeast, and the Emigrant Wilderness to the north.

The 1,189 square miles of the Park contain thousands of lakes and ponds, 1,600 miles of streams, 800 miles of hiking trails, and 350 miles of roads. Two federally designated Wild and Scenic Rivers, the Merced and the Tuolumne, begin within Yosemite's borders and flow westward through the Sierra foothills, into the Central Valley of California. Each year sees over three and a half million visitors, most of whom tend to cluster in the seven-square-mile area of Yosemite Valley.

Designated as a UNESCO World Heritage Site in 1984, Yosemite is internationally recognized for its spectacular granite cliffs, waterfalls, clear streams, groves of giant sequoia trees, and biological diversity. Indeed, about eighty-nine percent of the park is an officially designated wilderness. Although not the first region in the United States to be designated a national park, Yosemite was a focal point in the development of the concept, largely as a result of the work of people like Scotsman John Muir (see below).

## HISTORY

After Savage and Bunnell's incursion into the Valley, the history of the area continued in a rather tragic manner. Chief Tenaya and the rest of the Ahwahneechee were eventually captured, their village burned, and they were removed to a reservation near Fresno. Some were later allowed to return to the Valley, but rather prejudiced their return by attacking a group of eight gold miners in the spring of 1852. They fled and took refuge with the nearby Mono tribe. Then, after stealing some horses from their hosts, the Ahwahneeches were tracked down and killed by the Monos. (A reconstructed "Indian Village of Ahwahnee" is now located behind the Yosemite Museum, next to the Valley Visitor Center.)

The first-ever tourists were the entrepreneur James Mason Hutchings, artist Thomas Ayres, and two others. They ventured into the Valley area in 1855. Hutchings wrote articles and books about this and later expeditions in the area, and Ayres's sketches became the first accurate drawings of many prominent features. Photographer Charles Leander Weed took the first photographs of the Valley's features in 1859; later photographers included Ansel Adams, with his classic black-and-white images of the area.

Galen Clark, an early settler, was also an early conservationist. As a prominent citizen concerned by the effects of commercial interests, together with Senator John Conness (for whom the mountain was named), he urged protection of the area. A park bill passed both houses of the U.S. Congress and was signed by President Abraham Lincoln on June 30, 1864—creating what was called the Yosemite Grant. This was the first instance of land being set aside specifically for preservation and public use by action of the U.S. Federal Government, and set a precedent for the 1872 creation of Yellowstone as the first national park. Yosemite Valley and the Mariposa Grove were ceded to

**OPPOSITE** Snow field and North Peak, morning. Mount Conness.

**RIGHT** Skiers pause near the characteristic Clothespin tree, Mariposa Grove.

California as a state park, with a board of commissioners appointed to oversee the Park two years later.

Clark was appointed by the commission as the Yosemite Grant's first guardian, but neither Clark nor the commissioners had the authority to evict homesteaders (including the previously mentioned Hutchings) and the issue was not settled until 1875. Then, the homesteader land-holding rights were invalidated. Clark and the reigning commissioners were ousted in 1880, and Hutchings became the new Park guardian.

Tourist access to the Park improved in its early years and conditions in the Valley were made more hospitable. The truly significant increase in tourism occurred, however, after the first transcontinental railroad was completed in 1869. But the long horseback ride to reach the area remained a deterrent for many others. Then, three stagecoach roads were built in the mid-1870s in order to provide better access for the growing number of visitors to the Valley.

Scottish-born naturalist John Muir wrote articles popularizing the area and published papers on the area's biology, increasing scientific interest in it. Muir was one of the first to theorize that the major landforms in Yosemite were created by large alpine glaciers, bucking established scientists such as Josiah Whitney, who regarded Muir as an amateur.

Overgrazing of meadows—especially by sheep—logging of the giant sequoia, and other damage caused Muir to become an advocate for further protection. Muir convinced prominent guests of the importance of putting the area under federal protection; one such guest was Robert Underwood Johnson, editor of *The Century Magazine*. Muir and Johnson lobbied Congress for the act that created Yosemite National Park on October 1, 1890. The State of California, however, retained control of the Valley and the Mariposa Grove. Muir also helped persuade local officials to virtually eliminate grazing from the Yosemite high country. The newly created national park came under the jurisdiction of the U.S. Army's Fourth Cavalry Regiment on May 19, 1891, which set up camp in Wawona. Later, by the late 1890s, sheep grazing was no longer a problem, and although the Army had made many other improvements, the U.S. Cavalry could not intervene to help the worsening condition of the Valley or Grove. Consequently, Muir and his Sierra Club (which he had formed specifically as an environmental organization on May 28, 1892, in San Francisco) continued to lobby the U.S. government and influential people for the creation of a unified Yosemite National Park.

Then, in May 1903, President Theodore Roosevelt camped for three days with Muir near Glacier Point. On that trip, Muir convinced Roosevelt to

**OPPOSITE** Half-Dome and Yosemite Valley seen in the late afternoon from Clouds Rest.

take control of the Valley and the Grove away from California and return it to the federal government. Three years later Roosevelt signed a bill that did precisely that.

Also in 1903, a dam in the northern portion of the park was proposed. Located in the Hetch Hetchy Valley, its purpose was to provide water and hydroelectric power for San Francisco. Preservationists such as Muir and his Sierra Club opposed the project, while conservationists like Gifford Pinchot supported it. Then, in 1913, the U.S. Congress authorized the O'Shaughnessy Dam through passage of the Raker Act.

The U.S. National Park Service was formed in 1916, and Yosemite was transferred to that agency's jurisdiction. Tuolumne Meadows Lodge, Tioga Pass Road, and campgrounds at Tenaya and Merced lakes were completed in 1916. Cars started to enter the park in ever-increasing numbers following the construction of all-weather highways. The Yosemite Museum was founded in 1926 through the efforts of Ansel Adams and Franklin Hall.

In the early years of the Park, different companies ran multiple hotels and resorts. These resorts included the Wawona Hotel, the Yosemite Park Lodge, and Camp Curry, a tent cabin site in Yosemite Valley. The Yosemite Park & Curry Company was formed in 1925 to consolidate those often-competing concessions. The Park Service then granted the newly formed company exclusive right to operate hotels, restaurants, and most stores in Yosemite. In 1927, the new company was headquartered on the mezzanine level of its new Ahwahnee Hotel. The Yosemite Park & Curry Company then ran the concessions in the Park for over fifty years, until the company was sold in the late 1970s to U.S. Natural Resources (USNR), and a couple of years later sold again, to MCA, which operated Universal Studios. The Curry Company name continued during those ownership changes until 1993, when Matsushita acquired MCA. However, Manuel Lujan, the then Secretary of the Interior, objected to a Japanese firm operating concessions in a U.S. national park. As a result, and in order to avoid delay of federal approval of the acquisition, Matsushita arranged for the sale of the concessions company. As a result, ownership of its concession properties was transferred to the federal government, and the Yosemite Park & Curry Company name was finally discontinued.

More recently, preservationists persuaded Congress to designate 677,600 acres or 2615 square miles as the Yosemite Wilderness—the aforementioned eighty-nine percent that remains a highly protected area. Additionally, the Park Service has reduced inducements to visit the Park, such as the "Firefall," in which red-hot embers were pushed off a cliff near Glacier Point at night. Further, traffic congestion in Yosemite Valley in the summer months has become something of a concern and serious consideration has been given to the idea of excluding all cars that are not registered at a hotel or camping ground. The intention is to encourage summer, day-only visitors to travel by a free shuttle bus system, on bicycles, or on foot.

## GEOLOGY

Granite and remnants of older types of rock characterize the geology of the area. Its geological evolution and shaping started some 500 million years ago, when what is now identified as the Sierra Nevada region of California was submerged beneath an ancient sea. Sediments slowly built up on the ocean floor over the ages until they were thousands of feet in thickness and compressed the lower layers into rock. These great rocky layers, or plates, floated and moved slowly upon the Earth's molten, inner core. Then, about 200 million years ago, part of the Pacific plate slid under the North American plate—a process that is called subduction. Deep within the earth, tremendous heat and pressure caused the Pacific plate to turn into liquid rock or magma.

This magma rose toward the surface about one hundred to eighty million years ago but cooled while still underground into a huge block of granite, and by around fifty million years ago, the land destined to become Yosemite National Park was one of gentle, rolling hills and streams, including the slow-moving Merced River. On the hills and in the shallow valleys, the first hardwood forests developed and flourished. Slowly, starting ten million years ago and over a period lasting at least the next five million, the Sierra Nevada rose up to become California's "backbone." The Sierra block was lifted up and tilted westward, increasing the flow of the Merced River, which slowly but surely carved out the valley into a canyon, and the redwood forests started to flourish.

By the time of the Ice Age of three million years ago, the river had carved the canyon as deep as 3,000 feet (some 900 m), with its tributaries cutting the land more slowly. The ever-lowering temperature and encroachment of the ice started to thin out the forests as the Ice Age approached. From somewhere about a million years ago until 250,000 years ago, glaciers filled the V-shaped Yosemite Valley, widening, deepening, and carving it into a U-shape, forming hanging valleys from which waterfalls now cascade. Later, 30,000 years ago, the Yosemite Glacier entered the valley but did little to alter the landscape as the earlier glaciers had already excavated 2,000 feet into the bedrock. The ice gradually retreated and some 10,000 years ago, as temperatures continued to rise, the final remaining valley glacier melted. However, its terminal rocky debris or moraine dammed up the valley, creating Lake Yosemite. Slowly but relentlessly, the river sediment eventually filled the lake, creating the flat floor of the Yosemite Valley of today. Though geological process is perpetual and hard to envisage on a human time scale, the same process of sedimentation continues. At Mirror Lake, for example, it will not be all that long before sediment will completely fill in the lake, creating another meadow.

At the time of the Ice Age, the longest glacier in the Yosemite area ran down the Grand Canyon of the Tuolumne River for 60 miles (95 km), passing well beyond Hetch Hetchy Valley. The Merced Glacier flowed out of

Yosemite Valley and into the gorge of the Merced River, while the Lee Vining Glacier carved out the canyon of the same name and emptied into Lake Russell (a much-enlarged Ice Age version of what is now Mono Lake). Only the highest peaks, such as Mount Dana and Mount Conness, were not covered by glaciers. When the glaciers retreated at last, they often left huge rocky deposits—moraines—that impounded lakes such as the five-and-a-half mile long Lake Yosemite (a shallow lake that periodically covered much of the floor of what is now Yosemite Valley).

Almost all of the landforms in the Yosemite area are made up of the granite rock of the Sierra Nevada Batholith—a batholith being the geological name for a large mass of intrusive igneous rock that has been formed deep below the Earth's surface. However, a very small part of the Park, mainly in its eastern reaches near Mount Dana, is composed of metamorphic, volcanic, and sedimentary rocks. These rocks are called roof pendants because—believe it or not—they were once the gigantic cavern roofs of the underlying granite.

The various ways of natural wearing away—or forms of erosion—created joint and fracture systems that created the valleys, canyons, domes, and other features that are what we see today. The spacing between such joints depended upon the amount of silica in the granite and similar rocks—so that the more silica, the greater the tendency to create a more resistant rock, and larger spaces between joints and fractures. Features evident today, such as pillars and columns like Washington Column and Lost Arrow, as well as the dramatic Half Dome, North Dome, and inset arches like Royal Arches, are the result of these cross-joints.

The high country of Yosemite contains beautiful areas such as Tuolumne Meadows, Dana Meadows, the Clark Range, the Cathedral Range, and the Kuna Crest. Both the Sierra Crest Trail and the Pacific Crest Trail run through Yosemite, close by its most notable mountains—the red metamorphic rocky peaks of Mount Dana and Mount Gibbs, the granite peaks like Mount Conness, and the highest point in the Park, Mount Lyell.

The Tuolumne and Merced River systems rise in the Park along the crest of the Sierra Nevada and, over the ages, have carved out canyons that are 3,000 to 4,000 feet (900 to 1,200 m) deep. The Tuolumne River drains the entire northern part of the Park—an area of some 680 square miles (1,760 sq. km)—while the Merced River begins in the Park's southern peaks, mainly in the Cathedral and Clark ranges, and drains an area of approximately 511 square miles (1,320 sq. km).

The effect of water in all its forms—including the impact of glaciers, flooding, and resulting deposits—has been fundamental in creating the Yosemite landforms. The Park also contains around 3,200 lakes that each have a surface area of greater than 1000 square feet (100 sq. m). There are also two reservoirs and 1,700 miles (2,700 km) of streams, all of which come from the same two large watersheds.

Significant wetlands can be found in valley bottoms throughout the Park, and are often connected to nearby lakes and rivers through seasonal flooding and groundwater movement. High meadows—lying at 3,000 to 11,000 feet (900 to 3,500 m) in the Park—are generally wetlands, as are the river-based habitats found on the banks of Yosemite's numerous streams and rivers.

Yosemite is justly famous for its great profusion of waterfalls in a relatively small area. The many sheer drops, glacial steps, and hanging valleys are ideal places for waterfalls, especially during the key months when the winter snow is melting—April, May, and June. Located in Yosemite Valley, the 2,425-foot-high (739 m) Yosemite Falls is the highest waterfall in North America. Also in the valley is the much lower volume Ribbon Falls, which has the highest single vertical drop, 1,612 feet (492 m). Perhaps the most prominent of the Yosemite waterfalls is Bridalveil Fall, which is the waterfall seen from the Tunnel View viewpoint at the eastern end of the Wawona Tunnel. Wapama Falls in Hetch Hetchy Valley is another notable waterfall. Hundreds of other waterfalls also exist in the Park.

## ECOLOGY

Ecologically speaking, Yosemite is one of the largest and least fragmented habitat blocks in the Sierra Nevada, and the park supports a diversity of plants and animals. The park has an elevation range from 2,000 to 13,114 feet (600 to 4,000 m) and contains five major vegetation zones: chaparral/oak woodland, lower montane, upper montane, sub-alpine and alpine. About 50 percent of California's 7,000 recorded plant species occur in the Sierra Nevada and more than 20 percent within Yosemite itself. In turn, of these more than 160 are designated as truly rare plants, with equally rare local geologic formations and unique soils characterizing the restricted ranges that many of these plants occupy.

With habitats ranging from thick, foothill chaparral to expanses of alpine rock, Yosemite National Park supports over 250 types of fish, amphibians, reptiles, birds, and mammals. This wide range of species exists not only because of the many habitats in themselves, but also because most of them remain more or less intact—that is compared to areas outside the Park where human activity has resulted in habitat degradation or destruction.

## Flora

Along much of Yosemite's western boundary, habitats are dominated by mixed coniferous forests of Ponderosa and sugar pines, incense cedar, white, and

**OPPOSITE AND LEFT** The flora of the area is impressively diverse, from the very big—such as this giant sequoia in Merced Grove (opposite)—to smaller varieties such as the Spreading Phlox and corn lillies (top left and below left respectively).

Douglas firs—and the small in number but world-famous giant sequoias—interspersed with areas of both black and canyon live oaks. This lower ground also has a relatively mild climate, which goes a long way in explaining the relatively high diversity of wildlife.

Going higher, the coniferous forests—mainly red firs and pines, such as the western white, Jeffrey, lodgepole, and occasional foxtail white—provide a much more limited habitat and so fewer wildlife species occur here, becoming even sparser as one climbs even higher. Here, the few trees are much smaller and grow only in isolated stands broken by areas of exposed granite.

Even higher is the treeline, where a few remaining stands of lodgepole and whiteback pines and mountain hemlock give way to vast expanses of granite and a severe, alpine climate. It is a harsh, treeless landscape and very few wildlife species are adapted to life in such extreme conditions.

Contrastingly, the Park's meadowland can be found over a surprising range of altitudes. These meadows are vital habitats for wildlife. Animals come to feed on the green grasses and use the flowing and standing water found there. As a result, predators are also attracted to the meadows. Overall, the boundary between meadow and forest is attractive to many kinds of mammals and birds because of both open meadow areas for foraging and nearby cover for protection.

Looking in more detail at the trees, Yosemite's diverse landscape shelters nearly forty native types. Without question, the most famous of all are the giant sequoias. As well as being considered the largest living things on our planet, these trees can live from 1,000 to 3,000 years. The sequoia's three main growing areas are located in the Park—Mariposa Grove (200 trees), the Tuolumne Grove (25 trees), and the Merced Grove (20 trees). However, it seems that even in the relatively clean Yosemite air, atmospheric pollution is causing tissue damage to the giant sequoias, making them more susceptible to insect infestation and disease. Because the cones of these massive trees require fire-affected soil in which to germinate, the suppression of wildfires in the Park over previous decades has almost certainly reduced the trees' ability to reproduce. Thus—and rather ironically—a policy of deliberately controlled fire setting was introduced in the hope of helping germination and new growth.

Some of the other plentiful tree types include the California black oak—large deciduous trees, with yellow–green leaves and dark trunks—and the evergreen Ponderosa pine, with bark of irregularly shaped plates separated by dark furrows. The Park's other prominent trees are the incense cedars, which

have feathery, reddish bark and grow abundantly throughout the immediate area and the entire Sierra Nevada.

Of the hundreds of species of native wildflowers, many of which can be found only in the Park, the Mariposa lily is one of the most characteristic. It can be recognized by its three, white petals and dark center and is often found blooming under pine trees. In fact, springtime in the Park's meadows provides a magnificent display of other wild blooms such as the pink-to-white, dart-like flowers of the aptly named shooting star. The perennial herbs, shrubs, and trees—such as the dogwood and redbud—are mostly found only below 2,600 feet (around 800 m) and blooming between April and July.

There are also more than 130 non-native plant species that have now been recorded as growing on the Park's boundaries. These non-native plants were introduced into Yosemite with the migration of early settlers in the late 1850s. Natural changes and human activity have contributed to a rapid increase in their spread and a number of these species have become very aggressive, invading and displacing the native plants. This has a direct impact upon the Park's resources, as non-native plants can bring about significant changes to ecosystems by altering the inherent plant communities and the processes that support them. Some "invaders" cause an increase in the likelihood of fires, while others increase the available nitrogen in the soil and allow more non-native plants to become established. Also, many non-indigenous plants, such as the yellow star thistle, are able to produce a long taproot that allows them to out-compete the native plants for available water. Even by the 1940s, the bull thistle, common mullein, and Klamath weed or St. John's Wort were all identified as being noxious pests in Yosemite, with more recent ones such as the previously mentioned yellow star thistle, sweet clover, blackberry, and periwinkle already added to the list of plants that need to be rigorously controlled.

## Fauna

Keen birders, amateur birdwatchers—or even visitors with just a general interest in wildlife—can see over 150 different species of birds in Yosemite, all on a regular basis and all as a result of its substantially wide area and range of altitudes. In addition, around eighty additional species have also been spotted from time to time. Of those 150 regularly occurring species, about 80 percent are known (or estimated) to breed in the Park.

Because of the seasonal climate and temperature changes, most birds migrate to lower altitudes or move south in the late summer and fall. For example, of the eighty-four species known to nest in Yosemite Valley itself, over half are rare or absent in winter, with even fewer to be found in the higher habitats. Unfortunately, as so often seems to be the case these days, there has been a noticeable decline in the populations of quite a number of birds in the whole Sierra Nevada, including Yosemite. Possible causes include grazing, logging, fire suppression, development, recreation, pesticides, habitat destruction on wintering grounds, and (probably) overall planetary climate changes.

**RIGHT** Olmsted Point at sunset.

Curiously, though, a particular decline in a few species—such as the willow flycatcher—can be laid fairly and squarely at the door of another bird: the brown-headed cowbird. This non-native species is a natural parasite, laying its eggs in the nests of other species, usually songbirds. Then, when the cowbird eggs hatch before those of their host species, the larger, more vigorous cowbird chicks eject the eggs (or young) of the host species or compete with the host's young for food—behavior very similar to that of the Eurasian cuckoo.

In addition, for this and other songbirds, destruction of their willow and meadow habitat is also thought to be a cause of their decline. In fact, it is also recognized as the reason for the losses across the whole of the Sierra Nevada. Though many suitable habitats can still be found in Yosemite, the factors that have decimated birds like the willow flycatcher across California have, ultimately, affected their populations in the Park.

The brown-headed cowbirds are not the only avian "invaders," however, as two other non-native bird species in Yosemite have also been causes for concern. White-tailed ptarmigan were introduced for hunting into the east side of the Sierra in the 1960s and have expanded their range into Yosemite, occupying wide areas of alpine habitat. Also, along the Park's western boundary, wild turkeys, similarly introduced into California as game birds, seem to be having adverse effects on native plants and animals.

Research and data collection have continued in Yosemite in order to help protect its birds. Programs have included the monitoring of peregrine falcons, a bird whose numbers were decimated in the period of the 1940s through 1960s by the effects of the pesticide DDT. Peregrines only recently staged a recovery after the 1972 banning of this pesticide.

The great gray owl has also had its habitats surveyed, along with the distribution of California spotted owls in the Park. The great gray owls are of special interest in Yosemite because it is the furthest southern extent of their global range, and even there they are isolated by hundreds of miles from the next closest population in far northern California.

Twelve amphibian and twenty-two reptile species are found in Yosemite. The Park's amphibians include one type of newt and several salamanders. They have tails and resemble lizards, spending most of the year hidden away in order to escape the hot dry summers. They live under rocks or rotten logs or underground in damp crevices and burrows, emerging mainly in fall after the first heavy rains. Although the California newt is the area's only newt species, it is actually one of the Park's most visible amphibians, often seen in early spring, moving like a lizard in slow motion crossing roads or trails on their way to breed in rivers and streams. Of the four salamanders, the Lyell salamander is unique to the region.

The Park's other amphibians are the western toad, its close and endemic

relative the Yosemite toad, and five species of frogs. The most common of the frogs is the seemingly ubiquitous Pacific tree frog. Found at nearly all altitudes and in nearly all habitats, this tiny creature is the frog most commonly heard calling in springtime around the Park's meadows and ponds.

In marked contrast to the amphibians' preference for moist, damp habitats, Yosemite's reptiles—turtles, lizards, and snakes—prefer dry, rocky places. The lone turtle species, the western pond turtle, is an uncommon resident of mid-altitude ponds and slow-moving streams.

Of the eight varieties of lizards, the western fence lizard is the most numerous and commonly seen when darting across granite slabs or heard as they skitter through dry leaves. They are easily recognizable as the lizard doing the "pushups" that are their common display behavior. The northern and southern alligator lizards are almost as common as the western fence lizard—but as they tend to hide under rocks and logs, this makes them less obvious to the usual Park visitor.

There are thirteen kinds of snakes in Yosemite. The most common are three species of garter snakes , which live in and around ponds and wet meadows, where they hunt for small fish and frogs. The mountain king snake—with red, black, and cream-colored bands encircling its body—is the Park's most visually beautiful snake. In stark contrast, the rubber boa looks like some sort of giant earthworm, with its light gray color and blunt tail.

The remaining kinds of snakes are categorized as being uncommon-to-rare, mainly inhabiting the warm, dry lower elevations of the park. Of these, only the western rattlesnake is venomous. Nevertheless, snakes are an important part of the Park's ecosystem as they help keep the Park's rodent numbers in check. Fortunately, for the usual tourist, the likelihood of encountering one is relatively low; hikers and climbers simply need to pay attention in dry, rocky places and avoid putting their hands in holes or on ledges where snakes may be sunning themselves.

Yosemite is home to ninety mammal species. These include seven species of shrews and one mole that make up the insect eaters. Also in the Park, while four different kinds of hare and rabbit can be found, there is only one species of pika. For most visitors, many of Yosemite's mammals—like the mule deer and gray squirrels—are fairly common and can be seen nearly every day. Others, like the wolverine and Sierra Nevada red fox, are extremely rare and might be sighted only once a decade. Declining populations or a lack of hard information about their distribution and abundance has resulted in seventeen of the Park's listed mammals being designated as having "special status" by either the federal or California state government.

Bats and carnivores number seventeen and nineteen species each, and although often overlooked because of their nocturnal habits, bats represent a large proportion of the park's mammalian fauna. The mobility of these flying mammals enables them to occupy a wide range of habitats. They are found from the lowest elevations in the park to over 10,000 feet. They roost in rock

crevices and caves, under loose bark and bridges, in attics and tree cavities. North America's largest bat species, the western mastiff, is a Yosemite resident, as is the spotted bat with its huge ears and vivid white spots. These are the only two species in Yosemite whose echo locating calls are audible to the human ear.

Carnivores—the black bear, bobcat, mountain lion, raccoon, coyote, foxes, weasels, and skunks—are perhaps the most widely recognized group of mammals in Yosemite. Even the day visitor can see the Park's seemingly most nonchalant carnivore, a coyote that seems to stroll into parking and picnic areas simply to be photographed and grab a snack or two before wandering off again into the nearby trees.

Of the larger carnivores, bears remain the most important, in all manner of ways. When Euro-Americans arrived in California, grizzly bears inhabited most of the state, including the area that is now Yosemite National Park. However, the grizzlies were perceived by the settlers as a dire threat to life and property and were killed in large numbers. By the early 1900s, few grizzlies were left in the state. The last known grizzly bear in California was killed in the Sierra foothills, south of Yosemite, in the early 1920s. Their surviving cousins, the black bears, deserve a special mention. They are important animals, an iconic Californian motif and an integral part of the Sierra Nevada ecosystem. One of the many animal species protected in Yosemite National Park, black bears feed on a wide variety of natural foods, including grasses, insects, berries, and acorns; one estimate has it that there are roughly 300 to 500 individuals in the Park. Despite their name, most black bears in Yosemite are not black in color at all. Most are some shade of brown, ranging from almost blond, to reddish brown, to a dark chocolate. So, in terms of color, truly black bears are relatively rare. An individual bear's weight can change a lot through the year. Before entering winter hibernation, a bear's weight can be double what it was when it emerged from its den the previous spring—that is, if food is plentiful and rich enough. In fact, the largest black bear ever captured in Yosemite weighed 690 pounds (375 kg). Although black bears in Yosemite have caused hundreds of thousands of dollars in property damage, as they seek food rather recklessly and inadvisably stored in vehicles, the history of interactions between humans and black bears in Yosemite is both long and marked by some periods that one might now look upon as shameful. Early in the Park's history, little was done to keep bears from becoming conditioned to human food. Garbage was readily available in developed tourist areas, and little was done to discourage visitors from feeding bears. Indeed, the National Park Service maintained several "bear pits" in the park where the animals were fed garbage in an attempt to keep them out of park campgrounds and lodging areas—as well as to provide visitor entertainment. As a result, human injuries were not uncommon, and many bears were killed in the spurious name of public safety. So, it is both laudable and appropriate that attitudes changed over the years, with the emphasis now being on managing the behavior of humans rather than the

behavior of bears. All outdoor garbage cans and dumpsters are bear-resistant. All campsites, parking lots, and major trailheads are equipped with bear-proof food storage lockers that allow visitors to remove food from their cars and store it safely away from bears. In recent years, increased Park staffing has allowed more patrols to detect and correct food storage problems and to provide visitor education.

Also, all Park employees (of the National Park Service, concession-holders, and other partners) have accepted a larger role in protecting the bears. As a result, human-bear incidents and property damage declined by nearly 90 percent since the mid-2000s.

## CLIMATE

The weather in Yosemite is fairly predictable all year round. In the summer months—approximately June–September—it is typically sunny. The spring can be rainy and chilly, while the winter can be somewhat turbulent, with storms often seeming to come rapidly from nowhere. Summer temperatures are at their highest and rainfall is rare in the months of July and August. Nevertheless, the summer nights can become quite chilly with temperatures ranging from high to low. Rain can be expected along with some snow in late fall and early spring. Winter weather is almost as predictable as that of summer. Typically, there are snowy, rainy days and much lower overall temperatures. For the visitor, it is a time to wear heavier clothing and stay close to populated areas in case of sudden storms.

In terms of overall precipitation, the area has what is basically a Mediterranean climate, meaning that most rain and snow falls during the winter, and the other seasons are nearly dry. This increases with height, until it then begins to decrease slowly and gradually, from around 8,000 feet (2,400 m) all the way up to the crest. The amount of rain can vary from 36 inches (915 mm) at 4,000 feet (1,200 m) to some 50 inches (1,200 mm) at 8,600 feet (2,600 m). Even in the high country, the snow does not stay permanently on the ground until November; but it then accumulates all through the winter and persists into March or April—and occasionally into early May.

Temperatures in the Park decrease with increasing altitude and any extremes are moderated only by the fact that Yosemite is about 100 miles (160 km) from the Pacific Ocean. An anticyclone nearly always sits off the California coast in summer, sending cool air across the Central Valley and toward the Sierra Nevada. The end result is the clean, dry air of the Yosemite

OPPOSITE Yosemite's fauna is what you'd expect in such a mountainous wilderness: coyotes (below), bears (top left), marmots (top right) and the occasional rattler (top center)!

**RIGHT** Yosemite is an adventure playground for climbers, here seen on the Snake Dike route, Half-Dome.

**OPPOSITE** Peaceful start of a new day—deer, meadows, and Pothole Dome.

area—although, in the hot, dry summer temperatures are moderated by frequent thunderstorms, along with snow that can persist into July. The combination of dry vegetation, low relative humidity, and thunderstorms also result in frequent lightning-caused fires as well.

## THE PARK TODAY

Most of those who enter the Park stay for just the day, and only visit locations within Yosemite Valley that are easily accessible via automobile. Traffic congestion in the valley is therefore a serious problem during the peak summer visiting season. A free shuttle bus operates year-round in the valley, and park rangers encourage people to use this system since parking within the Valley during the summer is often nearly impossible to find. Almost the entire Park, however, is highly protected wilderness without roads, allowing no motorized vehicles and requiring permits for overnight stays.

For the day-only visitor, the Park can be divided into five sections: Yosemite Valley, Wawona–Mariposa Grove–Glacier Point, Tuolumne Meadows, Hetch Hetchy, and Crane Flat–White Wolf. Numerous books describe the trails, and free information is available from the Park Service in Yosemite. Most park workers strongly encourage guests to experience portions of the park other than Yosemite Valley.

Open-air tours around Yosemite Valley and the Mariposa Grove of giant sequoias are available. Many people enjoy short walks and longer hikes to waterfalls in Yosemite Valley, or walks among giant sequoias in the Mariposa, Tuolumne, or Merced Groves. Others like to drive or take a tour bus to Glacier Point (summer-fall) to see a spectacular view of Yosemite Valley and the high country, or drive along the scenic Tioga Road to Tuolumne Meadows (summer-fall) and go for a walk or take a longer hike.

In addition to exploring the natural features of the Park, visitors can also learn about the natural and cultural history of Yosemite at a number of facilities, including the Yosemite Valley Visitor Center, the adjoining Yosemite Museum, and the Nature Center at Happy Isles. There are also two National Historic Landmarks: the Leconte Memorial Lodge (Yosemite's first public visitor center), and the world-famous Ahwahnee Hotel.

For the fit and agile, over 800 miles of trails are available to hikers—anything from the easy stroll to grueling hikes up several park mountains, to multiple-day backpack trips between late spring and early fall. However, all overnight trips into the backcountry require a wilderness permit and most require approved bear-resistant food storage.

For bicycling enthusiasts, rentals are available in the Valley; spring through fall, with more than 12 miles of paved bike paths available in Yosemite Valley. In addition, bicyclists can ride on regular roads. The law requires the wearing of helmets for any rider under eighteen years of age. However, off-trail riding and mountain biking are not permitted any place within Yosemite National Park.

Rock climbing is an important part of Yosemite, and the campground in Yosemite Valley known as Camp 4 was instrumental in the development of rock climbing as a sport. It is listed on the National Register of Historic Places. Climbers can generally be spotted in the snow-free months on anything from ten-foot-high boulders to the 3,300-foot-high face of El Capitan. Numerous groups offer rock climbing classes.

Many of the roads in the park close due to heavy snow in winter. However, Yosemite Valley is open all year long. Downhill skiing is available at the Badger Pass Ski Area—the oldest downhill skiing area in California,

offering downhill skiing from mid-December through early April. Much of the park is open to cross-country skiing and snowshoeing, with several back-country ski huts open for use. Wilderness permits are required for backcountry overnight ski trips.

Yosemite offers outdoor activities throughout all four seasons. Such activities are available for all and at just about every level of ability and experience: from easy self-tour bike rides to strenuous multi-day guided backpacking trips, from a first ski lesson to any rock climber's ultimate challenge. Each season in Yosemite has its unique character and a range of activities and attractions—from day-tourists, all the way to the most experienced outdoor enthusiasts or rock climbers.

Finally, all Yosemite visitors must follow the same important rule: "Be careful not to cause ecological damage or upset the wildlife."

# THE YOSEMITE VALLEY

**PREVIOUS PAGES** El Capitan Meadows, Black Oaks and Cathedral Rocks.

**RIGHT** Redbud in bloom and Merced River, Lower Merced Canyon.

**OPPOSITE** Newly leafed trees on an island in the Merced River, Lower Merced Canyon.

The Yosemite Valley is one of the natural wonders of the world. As you enter from the south it's almost impossible not to stop and gaze in admiration from Tunnel View. This is particularly true in winter when this road, the Valley itself, and Wawona remain accessible; snow causes total closure of the Tioga and Glacier Point Roads, often until late May. Even then, tire chains are sometimes still required and access to the Valley can be limited unless chains are fitted, whatever the vehicle type.

The Yosemite Valley tells the story of two rivers: the Yosemite that shoots from a hanging valley in a spectacular waterfall and the Merced that rises in the snowfields and glaciers on Mount Lyell and passes through the alpine lakes of Washburn and Merced, flowing quietly through tranquil meanders along the almost flat floor of Little Yosemite Valley. Then, suddenly, it steepens and accelerates down a chute and bursts forth from the cliff as the 594-feet tall Nevada Falls.

April and May are the perfect time to see the Park's waterfalls at their very best. As warmer weather begins to melt the snow, even the smallest creeks rush with water, with many small, unnamed waterfalls and cascades forming all along the Valley rim. Of the better-known waterfalls, Yosemite Falls is the highest measured waterfall in North America and a major attraction in the park, especially when in full flow in late spring. The overall 2,425 feet from the top of the upper falls to the base of the Lower Falls makes them higher than combined heights of the Sears Tower and the Eiffel Tower. The huge drop of Yosemite Falls makes it the sixth highest waterfall in the world—but with the discovery of Peru's Gotaca Cataracts, they now appear seventh on some lists.

Although it is the most remote of the major falls in Yosemite, Nevada is easily seen from Glacier Point. It is also possible to hike to the top of the falls, either by

following the river up past Vernal Falls, or by taking the Panorama Trail, which follows the cliff edges all the way from Glacier Point. There, just above the cascade, is a deep green pool. Despite fences and the sign that warns starkly: "IF YOU SLIP AND GO OVER THE WATERFALL YOU WILL DIE," hikers sometimes wade in and even occasionally swim there—and someone is swept over the falls almost every year.

Yosemite is nirvana for rock climbers. It is worth remembering that Half Dome was said to be "perfectly inaccessible" as late as the 1870s. That was until George Anderson pioneered a route in October 1875, making the first ever ascent by drilling iron eyebolts into the smooth granite. Nowadays, it may be ascended in several different ways. Thousands of hikers reach the top each year by following a trail from the valley floor. The final ascent is accomplished by following a pair of metal cables raised on posts up the peak's steep but somewhat rounded east face. This cable route was constructed in 1919, and followed closely Anderson's route. The Mist Trail climbs past both Vernal and Nevada Falls and continues into Little Yosemite Valley, then north to the base of the northeast ridge of Half Dome itself. While it can be completed from the valley floor in a single, though long, day, many people take a break by camping overnight in Little Yosemite Valley.

The other great climb in Yosemite is, of course, the granite monolith of El Capitan, one of the world's favorite challenges for rock climbers. Once considered impossible to climb, the 3,000-foot vertical rock is now the standard for what is termed "gig-wall climbing." It has two main faces—the southwest (to the left when looking directly at the wall) and the southeast. Between the two faces juts a massive prow which provides one of the most popular and historically famous climbing routes and which is known to aficionados as "The Nose."

**OPPOSITE, LEFT** Lupines and manzanita bloom in early summer.

**OPPOSITE, RIGHT** The raging spring waters of Cascade Creek are further evidence of the season's abundant flow-off.

**RIGHT** Islet of trees, Cascade Creek.

**LEFT** A classic winter time view of Yosemite Valley with the Merced River in the foreground.

**OPPOSITE** Cathedral Rocks and El Capitan Meadows from the base of Ribbon Falls.

**OPPOSITE** Three images of dog-wood growing beside the Merced River.

**ABOVE**  Bridalveil Fall and Leaning
Tower, late afternoon.

**RIGHT**  Bridalveil Fall with water
sprayed by wind gusts.

**OPPOSITE**  Leaning Tower, sunset.

**OPPOSITE** Bridalveil Fall framed by snowy trees with new leaves.

**FAR LEFT** Creek at the base of Bridalveil Falls.

**LEFT** El Capitan and Merced River reflection.

**LEFT** Oak trees in spring, El Capitan Meadow.

**ABOVE** Sun shining through trees in fall colors.

**ABOVE** Black oaks in winter fog, El Capitan Meadow.

**OPPOSITE** Winter brings a dusting of snow to the trees and the west face of El Capitan.

**LEFT** Cathedral Rocks seen from Sentinel Meadow.

**OPPOSITE** Cathedral Rocks with mist, winter dusk.

**FOLLOWING PAGES, LEFT** Cook Meadow, spring storm, looking towards Catheral Rocks.

**FOLLOWING PAGES, RIGHT** Sentinel Rock picked out by the setting sun above the valley fogs of late fall.

**OPPOSITE** An elm tree shows off the seasons.

**RIGHT** Lupines beginning to bloom on the floor of a pre-burned forest.

**FAR LEFT** Upper and Lower Yosemite Falls framed by pine trees. The total fall of 2,425 feet from the top of the upper falls to the base of the lower falls makes Yosemite Falls the highest waterfall in North America (sixth in the world)

**LEFT** Lower Yosemite Falls with moonbow (lunar rainbow).

**OPPOSITE** Yosemite Falls, fed by snow melt, is at its most thunderous in the spring. The falls become a drip in late summer or fall.

**OPPOSITE AND RIGHT** Sunlight passing through the spray of Upper Yosemite Falls creates a rainbow at its foot. The upper fall 1,430 feet is formed by the waters of Yosemite Creek which hurl themselves over the edge of a hanging valley.

**LEFT** Backlit Upper Yosemite Falls from Fern Ledge.

**FAR LEFT** In early spring, temperatures can still be low enough to form an ice crust on the walls of Yosemite Falls.

**RIGHT** Seasonal waterfall on Royal Arches with Half-Dome in the background.

**OPPOSITE** Mount Watkins at sunset, Mirror Lake.

**RIGHT AND FAR RIGHT** Aspens, pine trees, and cliffs in Ahwanhee Meadows in fall and spring.

**OPPOSITE AND RIGHT** The Merced River near Sentinel Bridge provides a perfect view of Half Dome and its reflection in the limpid waters.

**PAGE 62, TOP** Half-Dome seen through Indian Arch.

**PAGE 62, BELOW** This downed tree was found at the very top of El Capitan.

**PAGE 63** A panorama taken as a winter sun sets over Yosemite Valley.

**FAR LEFT** Yosemite Creek and summer afternoon thunderstorm cloud.

**LEFT** Pine tree and Half-Dome from Yosemite Point, late afternoon.

**OPPOSITE** Granite exfoliation North Dome.

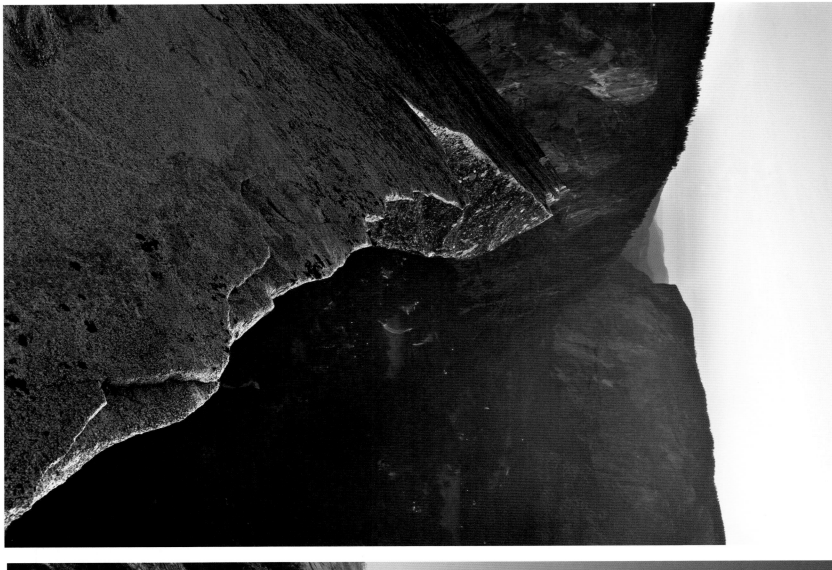

**FAR LEFT** The Diving Board and Yosemite Valley at sunset.

**LEFT** Last light on the northwest face of Half-Dome, from the Diving Board.

**OPPOSITE** A fine elevated view of Yosemite Valley and Half-Dome from Yosemite Falls Trail.

**OPPOSITE** Hiker looking down Yosemite Valley from Taft point at sunset.

**LEFT** Another sunset lights Half Dome.

**RIGHT** View of West Yosemite Valley showing, from left to right, Ribbon Fall, El Capitan, and Bridalveil Fall.

**OPPOSITE** Forest with snow, Chinquapin.

**FAR LEFT** Yosemite Chapel.

**LEFT** LeConte Memorial Lodge. A National Historic Landmark, it was built by the Sierra Club in 1903–04 and honors an early Director of the Sierra Club and University of California geologist Joseph LeConte, who died in the Valley in 1901.

**BELOW** The Ahwahnee Hotel, designed by architect Gilbert Stanley Underwood, opened in 1927. It sits below the cliffs of the Royal Arches rock formation.

**OPPOSITE** Yosemite Falls, Valley and Village seen from Glacier Point, dusk.

**OPPOSITE** Half Dome and Yosemite Valley viewed from Clouds Rest at sunset.

# THE MERCED RIVER AND THE SOUTH

**PREVIOUS PAGES** Merced River taking a turn over smooth slabs in Upper Merced River Canyon.

**RIGHT** Canyon near Merced Lake.

**OPPOSITE** Stream flowing over steep smooth granite, Lewis Creek.

The Merced River rises in the southeast of the Park and its headwaters start at around 8,000 feet. It is fed by a number of tributaries and lakes—such as Merced Lake near its headwaters. The largest tributary, South Fork, is some forty-three miles long and fed by rivers in the south of the Park such as Chilnualna Creek. As the Merced drops down it reaches the Little Yosemite Valley before cascading over Nevada and Vernal Falls on its way to the main Yosemite Valley. After meandering through the valley it leaves the Park near the West Entrance, after having been fed by Cascade Creek. It continues outside the Park until it joins the San Joaquin River.

The south of the Park is best known for Mariposa Grove, the largest stand of giant sequoias in the Park, with several hundred mature examples of the species. Two of its trees are among the fifty largest such trees in the world and the one named Grizzly Giant, at between probably 1,600–2,000 years old, is the oldest tree in the grove. Another, the Wawona Tree, included a tunnel wide enough for horse-drawn carriages and early automobiles to drive through. It was cut through it in the nineteenth century, but weakened by such a large opening at its base, it fell down in 1969.

Some of the other trees found in the grove that are worthy of special note include the Fallen Monarch, a tree that fell more than three hundred years ago; also, the Bachelor and Three Graces, a group of four trees, three of them growing very close together, with a fourth a little more distant, but with roots so intertwined that if one of them falls, it will almost certainly bring down the others; the Faithful Couple, a rare case in which two trees grew so close that their trunks fused together at the base.

Finally, there is the Columbia Tree, the tallest in the grove and in all of Yosemite; and the Galen Clark Tree that is supposed to have been the first of the giants seen by Clark upon finding the Grove in the mid-nineteenth century, and which inspired his love for these trees and drove his pioneering fight to set aside land for their eternal preservation.

**ABOVE** Stream in forest, Lewis Creek.

**OPPOSITE** Reeds and reflections, Merced Lake.

**LEFT** Merced Lake from above. The profile of Half-Dome can be seen in the distance.

**ABOVE** The length of the exposure shows the stars as lines reflected in the water below and enhances the clarity of the moonlit scene.

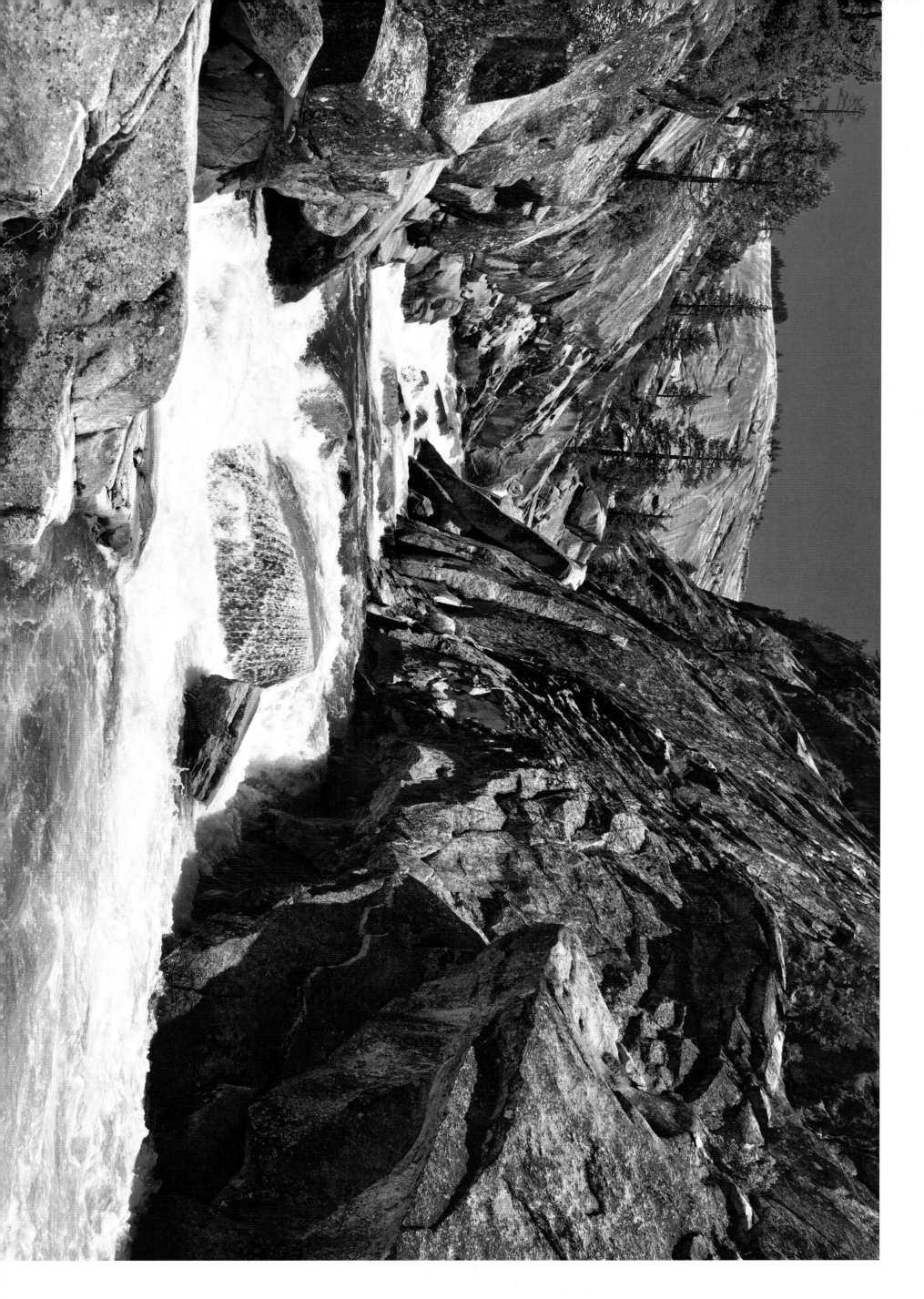

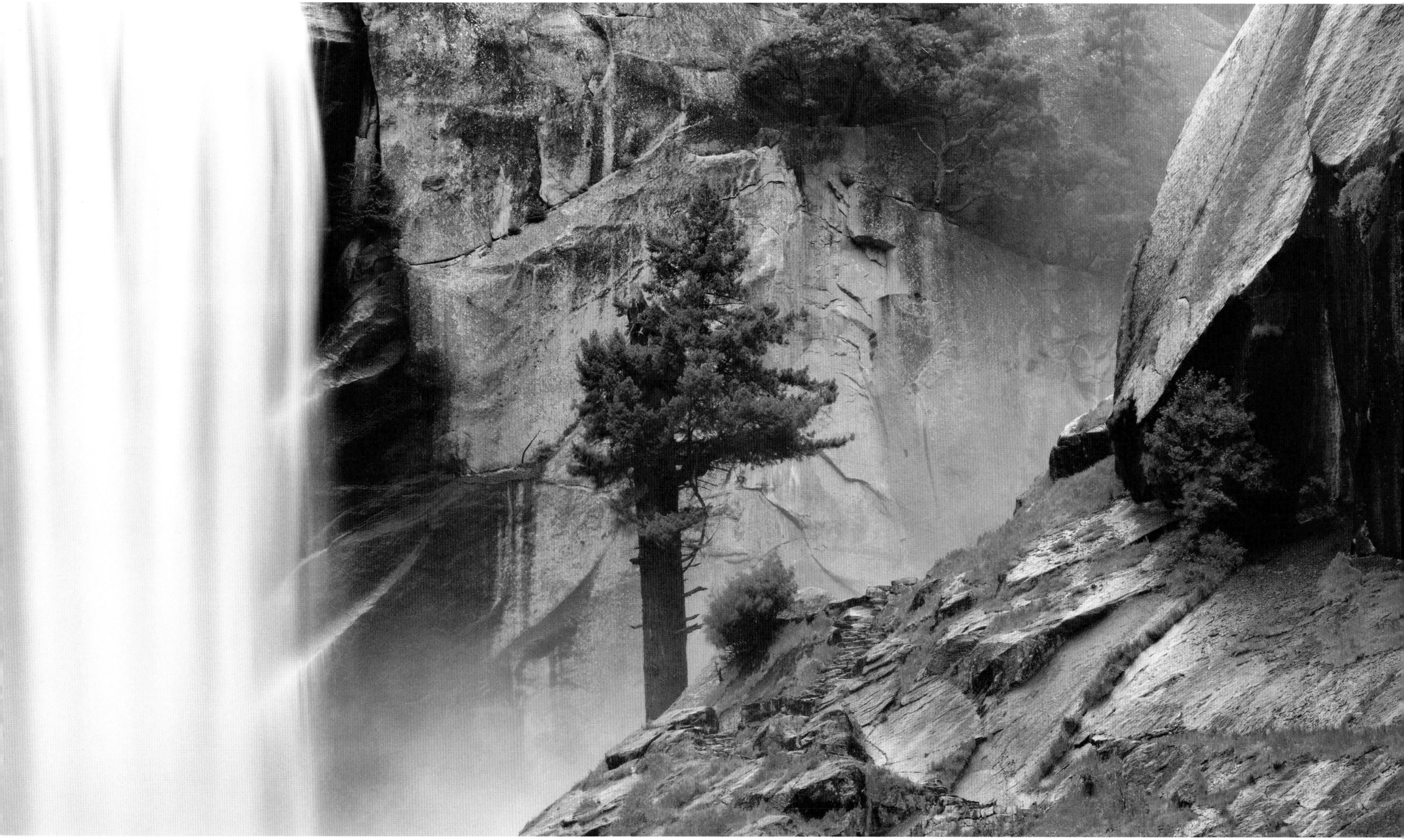

**LEFT AND ABOVE** Winter (left) and Fall (above) views of Vernal Falls illustrating the dramatic seasonal changes in water flow.

**ABOVE** The Merced at Happy Isles—the start of the Mist Trail to Vernal Falls and the long-distance John Muir Trail that goes all the way to Mount Whitney 211 miles south.

**LEFT AND OPPOSITE** Chilnualna Falls in the south of the Park is a dramatic series of five waterfalls.

**LEFT** Bachelor and Three Graces in Mariposa Grove—so intertwined are their roots that if one fell, all probably would.

**OPPOSITE** Mariposa Grove boasts two of the largest 25 trees in the world.

**LEFT** Mariposa Grove Museum at the base of the giant trees is almost hidden by the snow.

**OPPOSITE** A couple of Park visitors standing at the foot of the giant sequoia known as the Grizzly Giant are a revealing indication of the awesome size of this famous tree. It is 210-feet tall and some 2,000 years old.

**OPPOSITE, LEFT**
Wawona meadow, wild-flowers, and Wawona Dome.

**OPPOSITE, CENTER**
Pebbles in river and covered bridge, Wawona.

**OPPOSITE, RIGHT**
Sun through pine tree on edge of Wawona meadow.

**RIGHT** The Wawona hotel was built in 1876.

THE TUOLUMNE RIVER
AND THE NORTH

**PREVIOUS PAGES** Snow-covered Tuolumne Meadows and a big cloud sunset.

**RIGHT** The Lyell Fork of the Tuolumne River.

**OPPOSITE** The Tuolumne in Lyell Canyon at sunset.

The second of the two rivers of Yosemite is the Tuolumne. Another tributary of the San Joaquin, it is a little longer than the Merced. Its headwaters are high up—at some 13,000 feet in the southeast of Yosemite —in two forks, the Dana and the Lyell. The Tuolumne drains the whole of the northern half of the Park—a larger area than that by the Merced. North of the Tuolumne, the Park is crossed with trails and walks that are less well-traveled than the southern and southwestern areas.

The Dana and Lyell forks join in the peaceful terrain of Tuolumne Meadows, in the high (over 8,500 feet) country just south of the Tioga Pass Road. The tranquility of the lush meadows does not last, and soon the Tuolumne is cascading down to Glen Aulin over the California, Leconte, and Waterwheel Falls. The word "waterwheel" is well-chosen. Descending water—particularly in spring when swollen with melt waters—hits the granite below and bounces back upward where the wind whips it backward to rejoin the flow in a wheeling motion.

After all this excitement, the river passes through the Grand Canyon of the Tuolumne—a deep, "V"-shaped gorge cut through the rock since the last Ice Age—on its way to Pate Valley. From here it continues for trailless miles before tumbling into Hetch Hetchy Reservoir, the Hetch Hetchy Valley being notable for Wapama Falls. Beyond the reservoir's O'Shaughnessy Dam, the Tuolumne continues its journey, cascading and meandering through Poopenaut Valley before leaving the Park.

The Tioga Pass Road enters the Park in the west below the Tuolumne, running through Crane Flats and for some sixty miles across the Park, crossing the river at Tuolumne Meadows. It leaves the Park after the Tioga Pass—but it isn't open all year. Snow forces a seasonal closure when vehicles are not permitted between Crane Flat and Tioga Pass, including the Tuolumne Meadows area.

**OPPOSITE** Clouds colored by the setting sun reflected in a snow melt pool, Twolumne Meadows.

**ABOVE** Early spring sunset after spring thaw at Tuolumne Meadows.

**PREVIOUS PAGES, LEFT** Pine trees
in spring and Fairview Dome from
from Pothole Dome.

**PREVIOUS PAGES, CENTER** Grasses
and stream, late in a spring afternoon, Tuolumne Meadows.

**PREVIOUS PAGES, RIGHT** Looking
down on Tuolumne Meadows from
Fairview Dome on an autumn
evening.

**RIGHT** Fallen log and pond,
Tuolumne Meadows, sunset.

**FAR RIGHT** Tuolumne River and
distant domes.

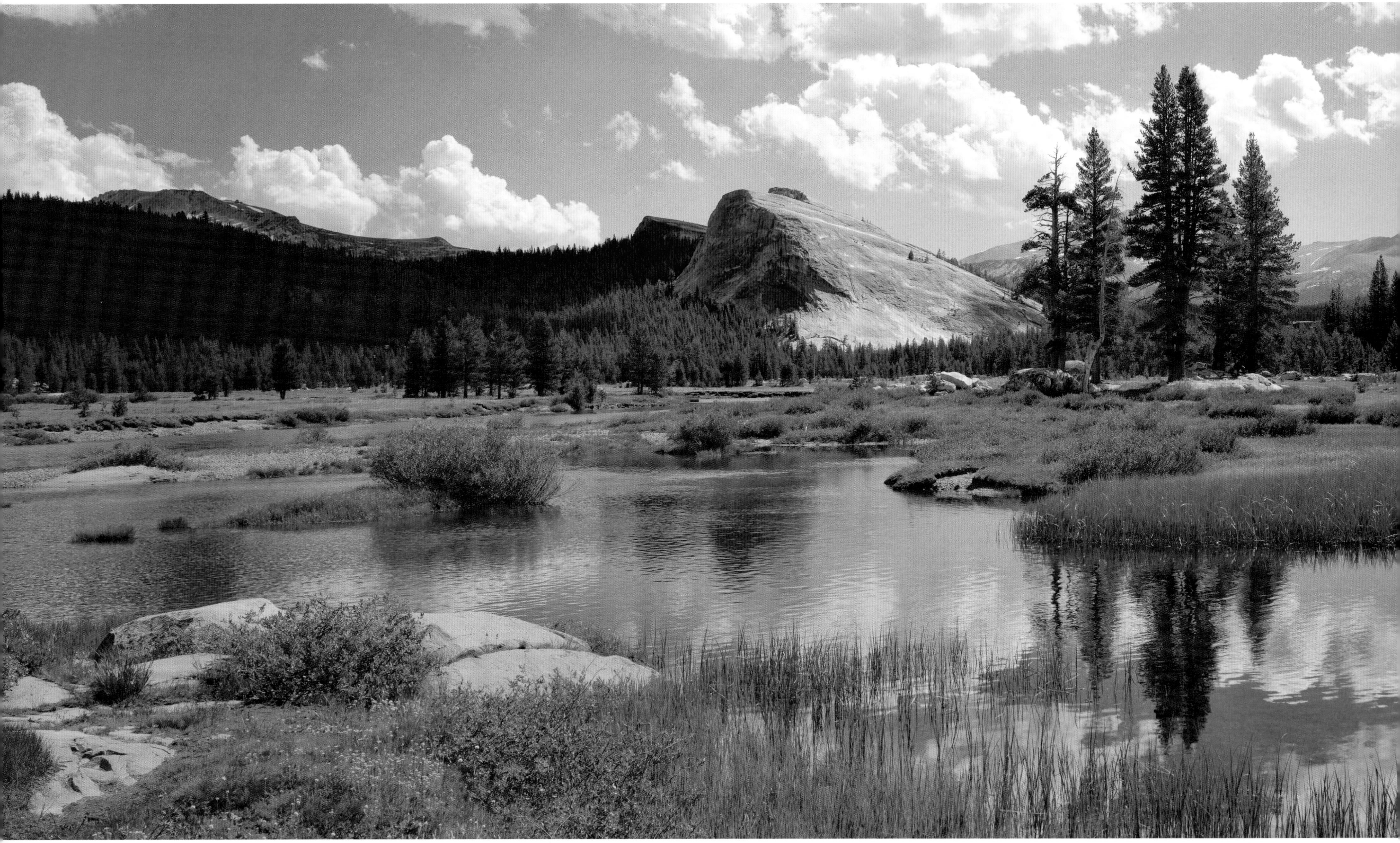

**LEFT** Lembert Dome reflected in seasonal Tuolumne Meadows pond.

**RIGHT** Wildflowers bring a dash of color to Tuolumne Meadows looking toward Lembert Dome.

**LEFT** Autumn mist near Tuolumne Meadows on an autumn morning.

**RIGHT** The Leconte Falls—one of two "waterwheel" falls produced as the water bounces back from the rocks.

**FAR RIGHT** The Tuolumne on its way to the Canyon of the Tuolumne.

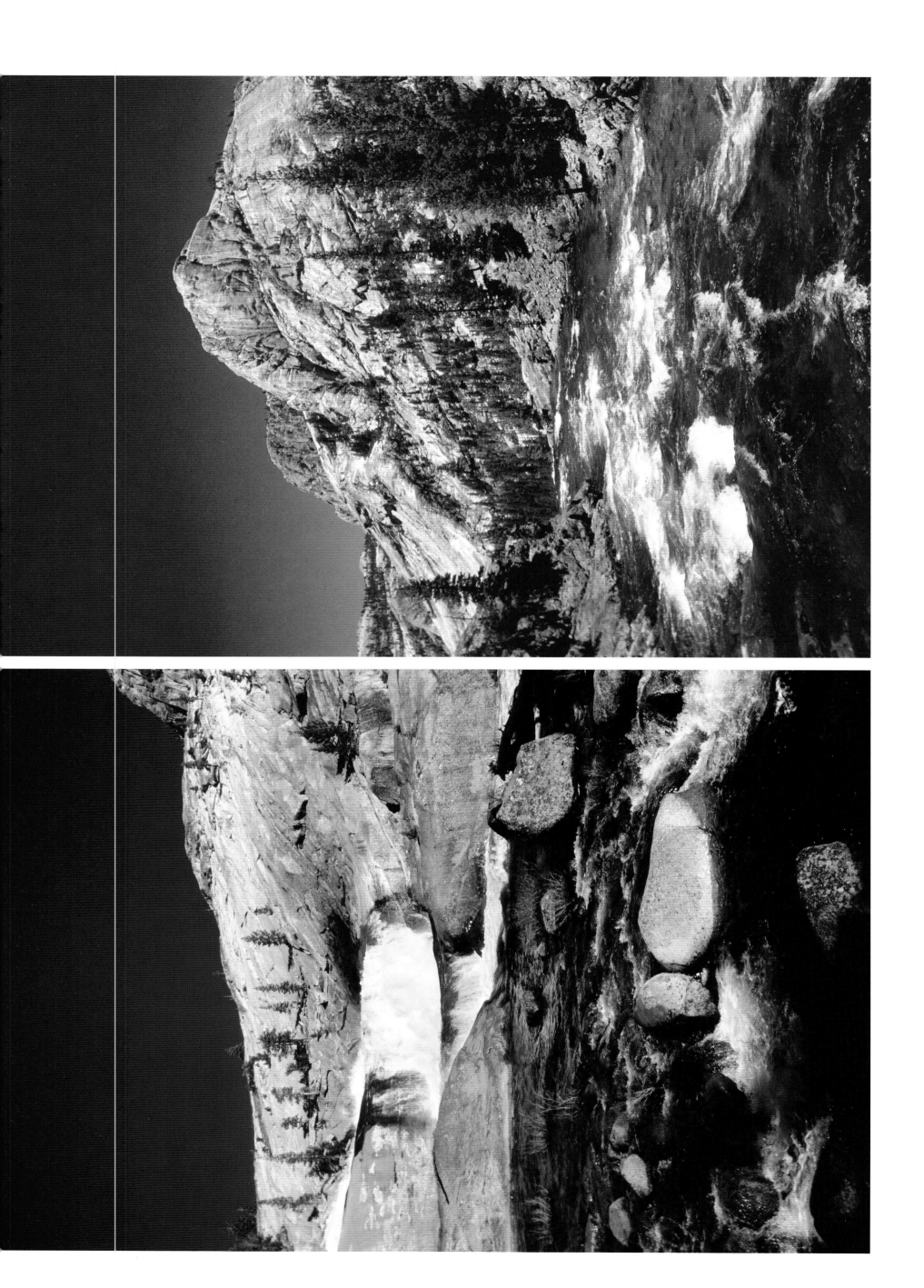

**OPPOSITE** LeConte Falls.

**RIGHT** Waterwheels at dusk.

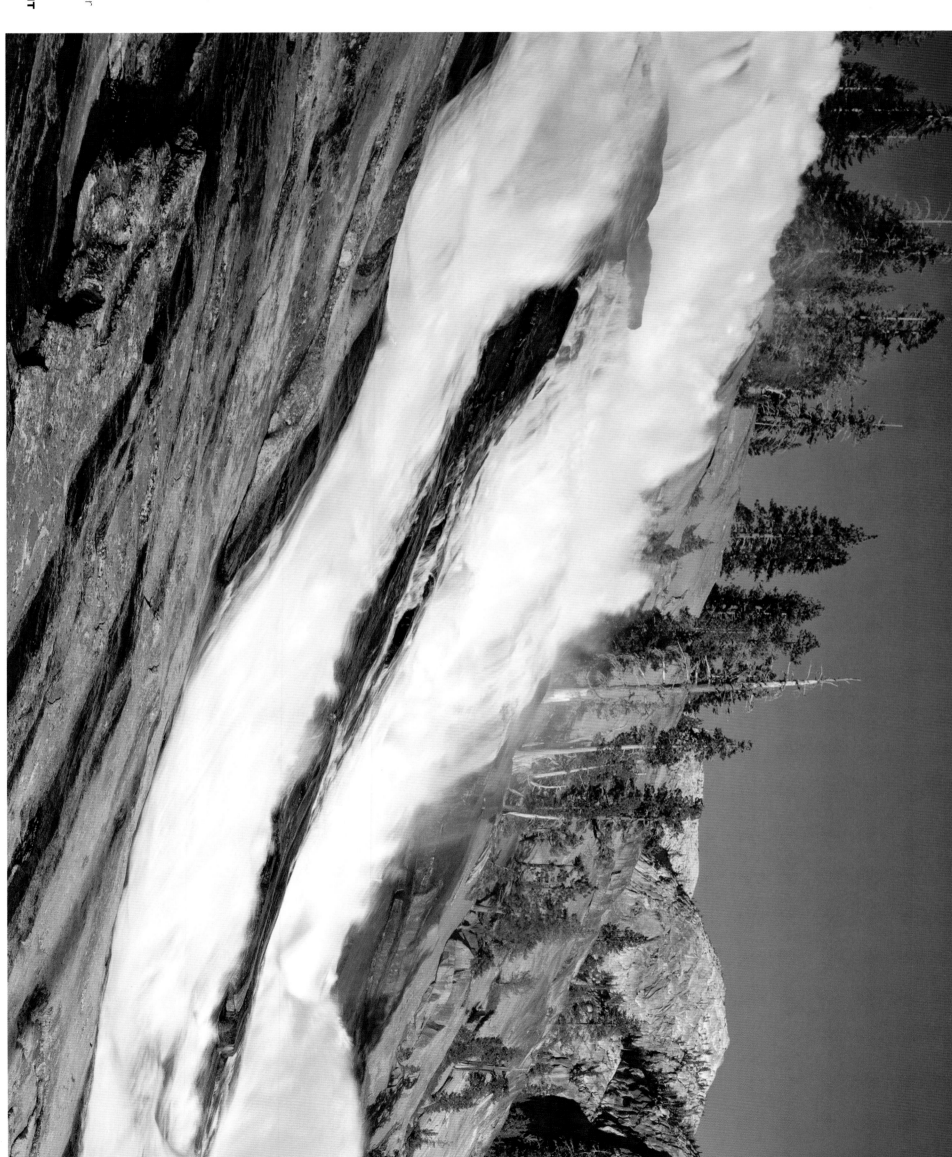

**FOLLOWING PAGES, LEFT**
Waterfall and pool at the
base of Wapama Falls.

**FOLLOWING PAGES,**
**CENTER** Wapama Falls
and rock wall, late summer
afternoon.

**FOLLOWING PAGES, RIGHT**
Hetch Hetchy Reservoir.

**LEFT** Upper Cathedral Lake and Cathedral Peak. Glaciers scoured away the granite to produce a basin for the lakes in this area.

**RIGHT** May Lake is a two and a half-mile hike from the Tioga Road.

**LEFT** Mount Hoffman sits high above Lake May.

**RIGHT** High country ridges at sunset, seen from the summit of Mount Hoffman.

**OPPOSITE** Cliffs on the north face of Mount Hoffman with a hiker to supply scale.

**FOLLOWING PAGES, LEFT** Slabs with Lyell Peak—the highest point in Yosemite (13,120 feet)—in the distance.

**FOLLOWING PAGES, CENTER** Evelyn Lake and trees.

**FOLLOWING PAGES, RIGHT** Fletcher Peak rising above Fletcher Lake.

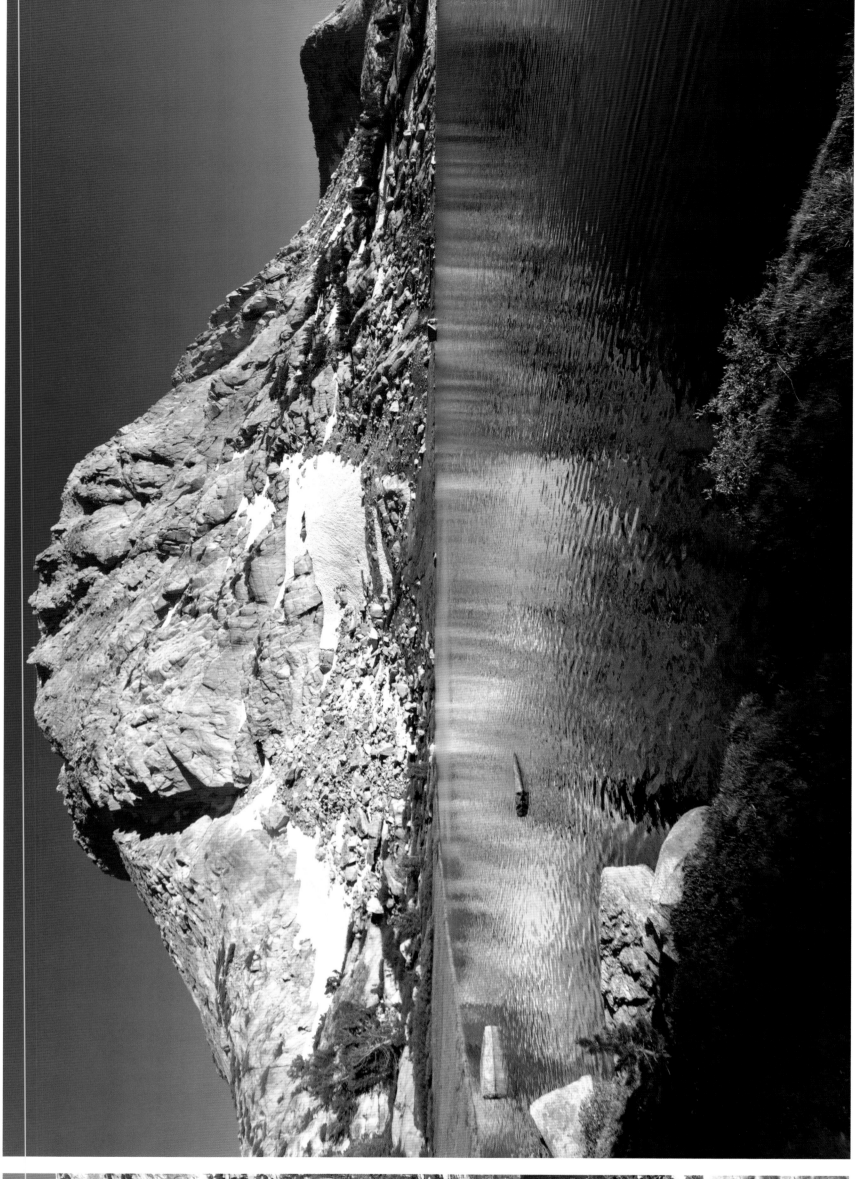

**FAR LEFT** Spires of Matthews Crest at dusk

**LEFT** Meadow below Tressider Peak

**ABOVE** Alpine lake in cirque at dusk, Vogelsang.

**LEFT** Flowers, Sheep Peak reflected in Roosevelt Lake.

**OPPOSITE** Rocky slopes of Mount Conness, dawn.

**BELOW** North Peak Boulders and Upper McCabe Lake, sunset.    **RIGHT** Upper Gaylor Lake.

**ABOVE** Pine and glacial erratics, dusk, Olmsted Point.

**RIGHT** Mountains reflected in partly iced Tenaya Lake, alongside the Tioga Road.

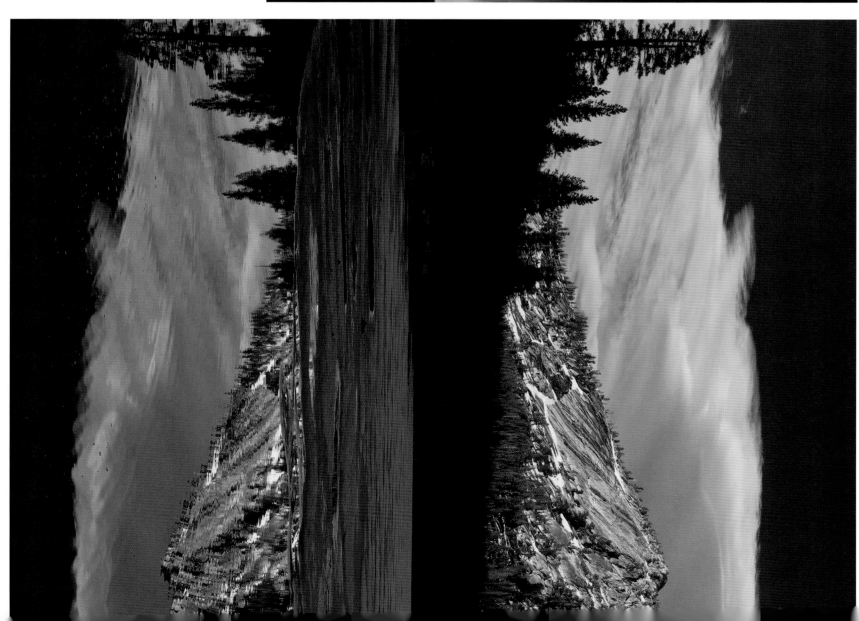

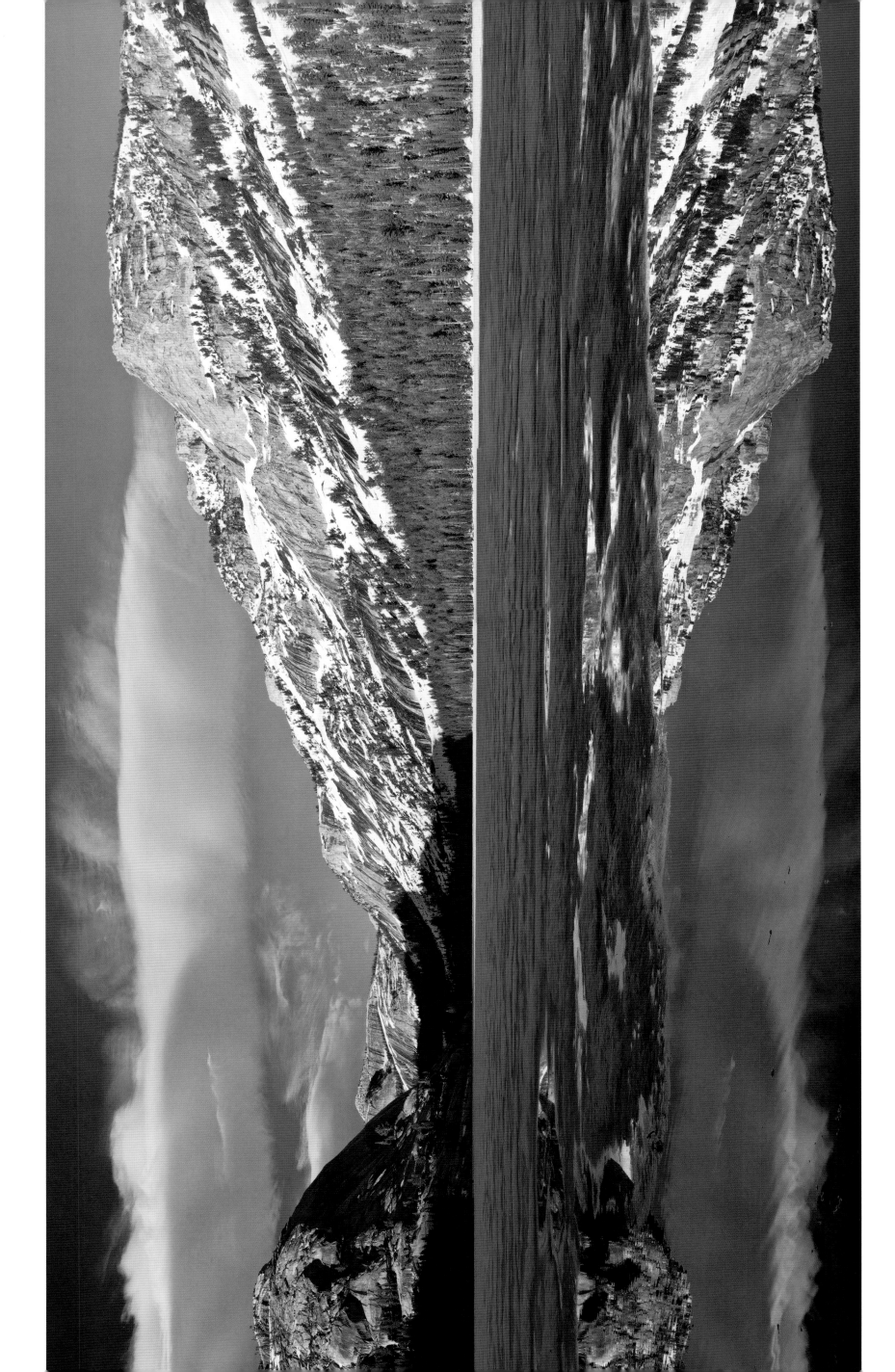

OPPOSITE Tenaya Lake in the spring.

**LEFT** Creek flowing in a snow-covered high country landscape. Mount Dana and Mount Gibbs can be seen in the distance.

**OPPOSITE** Alpine tarn near Tioga Pass. In the distance, Mammoth Peak.

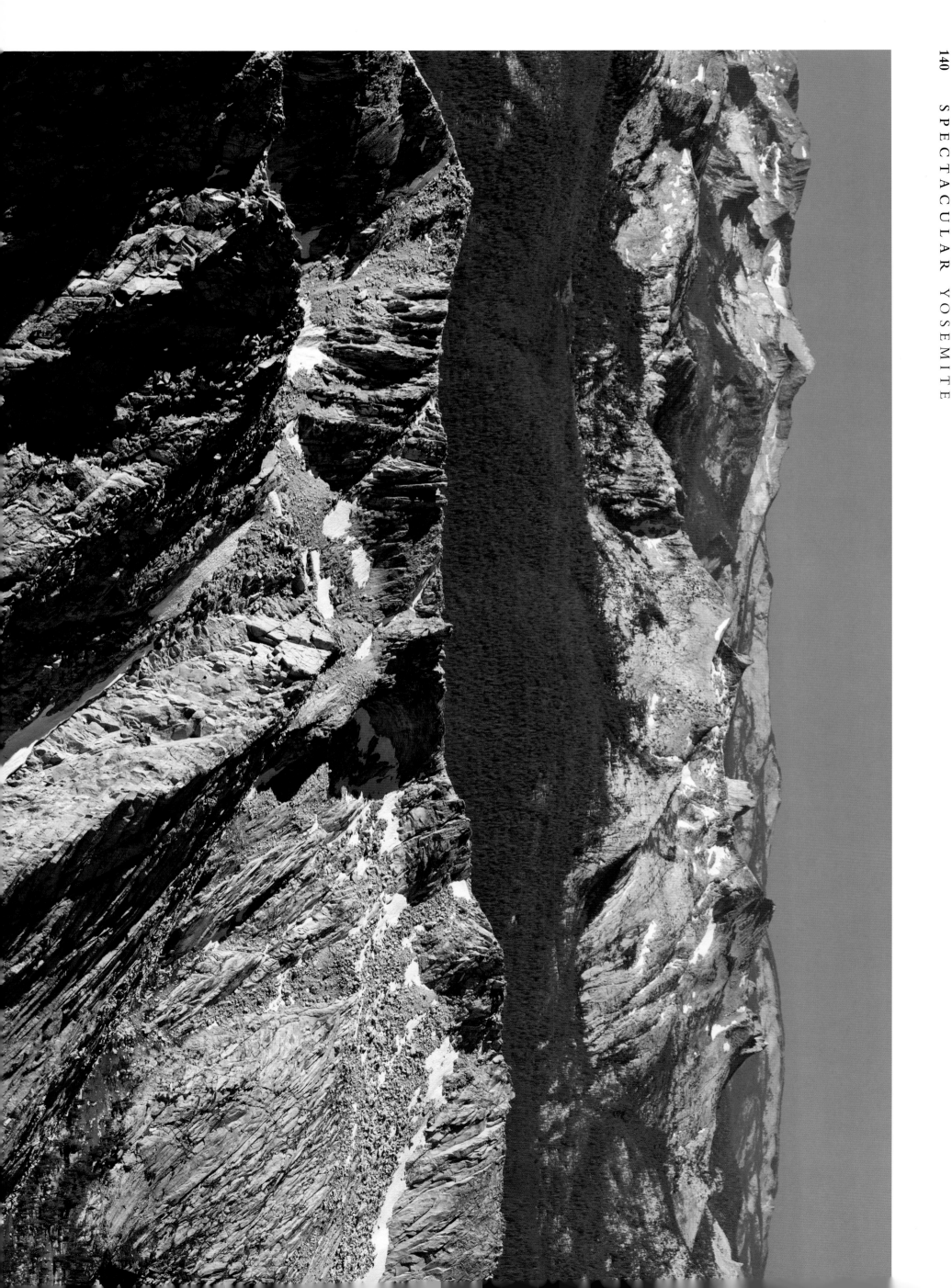

**LEFT** Looking toward the Yosemite Valley (in the background on the right) from Mount Conness with the Ragged Peak range and Cathedral Range in the distance on the left.

**OPPOSITE** Aerial view of Fairview Dome and Half-Dome from Mount Conness.

# INDEX